A Regency workbox, covered in red morocco leather, with a decorative gilt escutcheon and elaborate feet. The lid is tooled in gilt, has a carrying handle and is lined with a sepia print. The box contains an ivory pin poppet, a silk winder, two cotton barrels, a tapemeasure, a waxer and also ivory-handled tools and scissors. Most of these items are later additions, not the originals, but they are the correct type.

NEEDLEWORK AND EMBROIDERY TOOLS

Eleanor Johnson

The Shire Book

Published in 1999 by Shire Publications Ltd, Cromwell House,
Church Street, Princes Risborough, Buckinghamshire HP27
9AA, UK
(Website: www.shirebooks.co.uk)

British Library Cataloguing in Publication Data: Johnson,
Eleanor. Needlework and embroidery tools. – 2nd ed. – (The
Shire book). Needlework – Equipment and supplies –
History. I. Title II. Needlework tools. 646.1'9'09.
ISBN 0 7478 0399 4.

Cover: *A fine-quality Victorian fitted rosewood workbox, the lid lined with the original quilted sage-green silk, which is also used for the covered compartments. The box has the original complete set of mother-of-pearl tools and accessories. It is photographed with a selection of the collectable accessories featured and illustrated in the book.*

ACKNOWLEDGEMENTS
The author acknowledges with thanks the loan of the workbox on the cover from Lucy, and
of other items for the colour photographs from Audrey, Jean and Lynne. The photographs
on pages 3, 6, 7 (bottom), 18 (both), 22 (both), 23 (both), 25 (bottom left and right), 38 (bottom)
and 39 are by John Watson. All the other photographs, including the one on the front cover,
were taken by David A. Ross LRPS.

Printed in Great Britain by CIT Printing Services Ltd, Press
Buildings, Merlins Bridge, Haverfordwest, Pembrokeshire
SA61 1XF.

CONTENTS

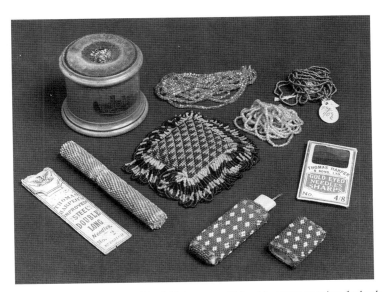

A collection of beadwork needlework items. (Top left) An unusual Mauchline ware container for beadworking; the top with the shallow cavity holds beads in use, for ease of picking up each one; this lid lifts off to reveal space inside for beads. To the right are three strings of the very small beads used. (Bottom left to right) A packet of needles; a cylindrical needlecase decorated with blue and yellow beads; a beaded fringed pincushion in two colours; a flat needlecase, the top removed; and another packet of needles.

INTRODUCTION

Needlework has a long history, as also have the more mundane tools associated with it: for example, pins, needles and scissors. In earlier times necessity was the mother of invention, and thorns were used for pins, fish bones and carved bone for needles, and primitive scissors were made of iron. Sewing was an essential part of daily life for the making of all clothes in skins and coarsely woven materials. Naturally, as time went on, improvements were made, both in the tools and in the fabrics used. Craftsmen were quick to use their skills in producing more efficient, attractive tools in more elaborate and expensive materials.

There are references to needlework tools from Roman times, but they increased greatly in the sixteenth, seventeenth and eighteenth centuries until, for our present purpose, the nineteenth century became the most prolific period in mention and manufacture. Changing modes of life and social customs elevated needlework from a pure necessity to an art and social grace. Women of the middle and upper classes had ample leisure, as servants did most of the work of running the household for them. Needlework and many similar activities were popular diversions for occupying their time. During Regency and Victorian times needlework, knitting and tatting were important social accomplishments for ladies in society. Tatting involved a graceful movement. Needlework required skill and provided scope for the exercise of good

Small sewing cases. (Top row, left to right) A leather-covered Ladies' Companion. A leather case with zip fastener, a souvenir of the Royal Netherlands Steamship Company, containing a brass thimble, scissors, a packet of needles, court-plasters and a skein of coloured threads. Another Ladies' Companion open to show the contents: the compartment at the back has a folding leather container for steel tweezers, a stiletto and a buttonhook; the next compartment in front contains a memo card, the front made of imitation ivory and the back imitation tortoiseshell, with a calendar dated 1889 and giving the name of the retailer; next there are scissors, and in the front compartments a pincushion, places for a pencil, a penknife, and a thimble in its recess. An oval French red leather-covered case lined in red satin, containing steel scissors and matching thimble decorated with gilt crosses. (Front row, left to right) A tiny leather-covered case (7 by 4.5 cm), open, with a clip fastener, lined in dark blue silk, containing matching miniature pinchbeck needlecase, scissors, thimble, bodkin and stiletto. A closed rectangular French sewing case covered in shagreen, with its silver stiletto, thimble, scissors and needlecase in front. An imitation leather-covered rectangular box, lined in red velvet, containing matching tapemeasure, double-ended pincushion, waxer and thimble, and a separate set of four gilt items, stiletto, needlecase, bodkin and scissors.

(Left) A hallmarked silver chatelaine, dated 1897, with three decorative chains ending in swivel clips, with a pencil, a heart-shaped pincushion and a note-book or aide-mémoire, which has ivory pages with elaborate silver covers. (Top centre, left to right) Three steel items for a steel chatelaine: a spherical tapemeasure with wind-in red tape, an acorn-shaped pincushion and a slim needlecase. (Bottom centre) Two nanny or sewing brooches, one with a yellow stone and one with a moonstone. (Right) Another hallmarked silver chatelaine, dated 1895, with a pen-knife, a scent bottle, one empty clip and a silver buttonhook with a blue lace agate stone in the handle. All the silver chatelaine items are of contemporary dates to the waist clips.

taste and ingenuity in the use of a wide variety of materials and patterns in the making of dainty and exquisitely conceived articles. Among these were miniature pincushions in patchwork and small purses.

The custom of taking needlework to large gatherings or private social occasions continued into the early nineteenth century. While those who preferred to played cards, it was quite polite for others to sit and chat and occupy themselves with their embroidery or other work. For this purpose ladies carried small sewing cases or 'étuis'; some are called the 'Ladies' Companion'. These came in a variety of sizes and materials and had a varying number of implements inside. Some of the pretty articles they had made or been given as presents would be included, especially needlecases and pincushions, and these would be passed round for admiring comment and as topics for conversation.

Ladies also carried small items with them when out visiting or shopping, especially pin wheels, in order to effect immediate repairs should a garment become torn. These were often concealed in large pockets in

their voluminous skirts or in little drawstring bags. They could also be worn on a chatelaine suspended from the waist by a large hook; the earliest of these were very decorative in cut and faceted steel, but these were later superseded by gold, silver and silver plate. The chatelaine had a number of chains suspended from the central clip, with a different item hanging at the end of each. There might be a thimble in a bucket, scissors

Workboxes and caskets. (Top row, left to right) A small burr-walnut box with bun feet and a lift-out pincushion lid, which has been re-covered; a rectangular mahogany reel box with a drawer in the base, open and showing the reels made of boxwood, fitted on to lift-out metal rods; a rectangular work basket with suede-covered lid and carrying handle, lined in brown satin. (Centre bottom) A small fitted cedarwood workbox of Middle Eastern origin, the lid inlaid with ivory and cut steel. (Far right) A small French fabric-covered work basket, with carrying handle decorated with gilt thread and two green velvet-covered pincushion lift-up lids.

in a sheath, pincushion, needlecase, pencil, buttonhook, scent bottle or notebook. In the earliest examples the chains terminate in a split ring, but later ones have a swivel clip to attach the necessary requisites. Chatelaines developed in medieval times, from the necessity for the lady of the house (after whom they are named) to carry the keys to her storage chests on her person. Tea and other precious commodities were kept safely in this way before the appearance of cupboards. They went out of fashion in the late nineteenth century but were revived by Queen Alexandra as a fashion accessory.

For the ladies so busily occupied with their various activities there were in the towns many shops that sold the accessories, or 'toys' as they were called, and the choice was wide. In the country pedlars or packmen visited homes offering the ladies of the household their various wares. In addition there were the popular annual fairs where goods were displayed in booths. Stourbridge Fair was one of the largest and most popular, not only with the local country people but also with ladies of fashion, who drove long distances in their carriages to visit them and stroll among the stalls inspecting the latest trifles.

In the days when the parlour was an important feature of the Victorian home, furnished with so many 'whatnots' and small tables, an outlet was readily to hand for all the delightful small articles made by the accomplished needlewomen. The dainty trifles they made were commonly given away as presents, which were then displayed for all to admire.

For use at home, many needlewomen owned a workbox elaborately decorated with brass, ivory or mother-of-pearl. Most commonly these are rectangular, with a loose lift-out tray divided into compartments and covering a space underneath for additional accessories or work in progress. During the early nineteenth century the tray was fitted with matching sets of cotton barrels, to hold cotton, together with pin boxes, thimble, tapemeasure, thread waxer and emery, as well as space for scissors and other tools. Later boxes had cotton-ball holders topped with mother-of-pearl, with the other items to match, or wooden cotton reels in the appropriate compartments.

During the Victorian era, with the coming of the railways and improved roads, travel and visits further afield became easier and more popular. The growth of the tourist industry followed, and the manufacture

Right: *Tunbridge ware needle-work items. (Top row, left to right) Standing, a needlebook with covers in small cube pattern, and flannel leaves inside; an early pincushion bowl with painted coloured rings and a pink pincushion; a rectangular box with mosaic veneer, having a sliding pincushion lid. (Centre row, left to right) A rosewood pin wheel covered in mosaic; a stickware combined waxer and pincushion; a mosaic pin wheel with a cut-out edge; an early cotton barrel (the spindle missing) with painted coloured rings. (Bot-*

tom row, left to right) A stickware pincushion and waxer without wax, showing the central spindle on to which the wax was fixed; an early tapemeasure with painted coloured rings and the original hand-marked silk tape; another similar one with a different winding handle.

Left: *Mauchline ware sewing items. (Clockwise from left) A rectangular cotton box with compartments for three reels inside; the print on the lid is of George Square, Glasgow. A saucepan-shaped tapemeasure with a print of the Auld Brig o' Doon. A round cotton box with holes in the side for the different threads to emerge; the print on the lid shows 'Teignmouth from the East Cliff' and there are other, smaller views of Teignmouth round the sides. A spherical wool-ball holder with hanging*

cord and a print of 'Barmouth from the sea'. A saucepan-shaped thimble holder, with the lid removed, and a print of 'Barmouth from the sea'. (To the left of this) A thimble-shaped thimble box, with a print of St George's Church, Doncaster. A French rare parasol-shaped needlecase, with the print 'Salon de Trouville'. (Above this) A small round pincushion with a print of Scarborough. A round pin wheel, with a print of Abercairny. An egg-shaped thimble holder, with the print 'Barmouth from the sea'.

Five needlework items in tartan ware, fea-turing Royal Stewart tartan. (Left to right) A trefoil-shaped pincushion; a case contain-ing three pairs of steel scissors; a round pin-cushion; a sloping-fronted box for packets of needles. (Bottom centre) A tatting shuttle.

7

Fernware and tartan ware sewing items. (Top row, left to right) A rectangular dark fernware cotton box, with holes in the side for the thread to emerge; a green and red pattern fernware needlebook lined in dark blue satin; a tartan barrel-shaped thimble holder; a tartan needle packet box with sloping lid; a diamond-shaped tartan pincushion. (Bottom row, left to right) A small round dark fernware pincushion; a double-ended pincushion with green and red fern pattern; a small round pincushion, also fern pattern; a tartan tatting shuttle.

of souvenirs was vastly increased. The variety of goods produced for this purpose is infinite, and among them are many of the items related to needlework so prized by collectors today and originally given as gifts by those who had visited the growing number of fashionable resorts.

There are several types of souvenir wares that the collector of needle-work tools may find. *Tunbridge ware* was made at Tunbridge Wells in Kent, and most of the pieces now turning up date from the early nineteenth century onwards. The earliest were decorated with painted coloured lines on light-coloured wood. It was followed by *stickware*, articles turned from a group of pieces of different-coloured woods glued into a stick. Then there was *mosaic*, fine slices cut from a similarly made stick and used to decorate wooden articles, much of the undecorated part being made of rosewood.

Scottish transfer ware or *Mauchline ware*, so called because it was first

Needlework items with colour prints under glass and mirrors on the backs. (Back row, left to right) A needlebook, with a print of Ann Hathaway's Cottage; a round pincushion, with a print of Salisbury Cathedral; another needlebook, the interior flannel leaf just showing, lined in red silk, with the print of a college and the coat of arms on the back cover; a round pincushion, with a print of St John the Baptist church, Frome. (Front row, left to right) A round pincushion with a print of Stonehenge; a needlebook, with a print of Osborne House; a round pincushion with a print of Blenheim Palace.

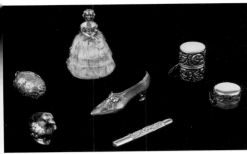

Left: *Needlework items made in silver. (Back row, left to right) An elaborately decorated egg-shaped thimble holder with a ring to hang on a chatelaine; a rare pincushion lady, the top body hallmarked silver, with a delicate printed silk frilled skirt; an American, finely decorated box to hold a reel of thread, having a hole in the side for the thread to emerge; a similar smaller example, also American. (Front, left to right) A small hallmarked silver bird with a blue velvet pincushion on its back; a hallmarked silver shoe also with a blue velvet pincushion; a slim hallmarked needlecase.*

Right: *Mother-of-pearl sewing items. (Far left diagonal row, bottom to top) A waxer, with the wax between two carved flat discs; a pincushion with a pink silk cushion (these two items, the tapemeasure to their right and the mother-of-pearl handled scissors are all from the fitted workbox on the cover); an egg-shaped thimble holder. (Next diagonal row, bottom to top) An-other egg-shaped thimble holder*

with a purse-type fastening; a tapemeasure with the original pink silk tape, winding in by a small handle on the top; a rectangular needlecase; and another needlecase with a carved fan top (these two are Palais Royal); a small plain needlecase; a tambour hook; and a needlebook with pierced cover featuring a bird. (Next diagonal row, bottom to top) A small round pincushion with a blue velvet cushion and a small silver engraved disc attached to the top; rare mother-of-pearl-handled scissors; a tapemeasure with a mother-of-pearl disc topping an ivory base. (Far right diagonal row, bottom to top) A small round waxer; two delicate silk winders; and two emeries with red silk emery cushions inside and different decorated tops.

Right: *Mother-of-pearl sewing items. (Left-hand group of five) Two cotton-ball holders, without cotton; these show the central brass spindle; the solid bottom rod on a bone circular base fits into a hollow rod attached to the deco-rated mother-of-pearl top. A small holder of a different type. Two cotton-ball holders with their original cotton; these two are from the fitted workbox on the*

cover. (Centre group) Seven different-sized mother-of-pearl silk winders of varied patterns. (Far right) Another group of cotton-ball or reel holders, showing different designs on the tops, photographed with two skeins of pure silk Filoselle thread of the type that would have been wound on to the winders.

Below: *Ivory sewing items. (Back row, left to right) A tapemeasure; a waxer; three cotton barrels; an unusual thread holder, both the top and bottom finely carved; and a small reel. (Centre row, left to right) An ivory stiletto,*

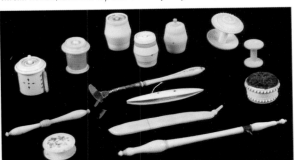

the fine steel pricker screwing into its pro-tective cover; an ivory-handled seam presser, with a tatting shuttle below it; a small round pincushion with a green vel-vet cushion. (Bottom row, left to right) A small round waxer with painted top; a rare pea-pod-shaped needlecase; and a tambour hook, the larger end of which unscrews to reveal the space to hold different sizes of hook, which when the other end is un-screwed can be fitted in to be held by the small winged screw on the side.

Needlework items in tortoiseshell piqué and straw-work. (Left to right) A fine needlebook with tortoiseshell and gold piqué covers and small gold cartouches for initials; a flat straw-work needlecase; another straw-work needlecase; and an oval pincushion in tortoiseshell with gold piqué decoration.

Sewing items in vegetable ivory. (Back row, left to right) A tapemeasure winding in by means of the ivory knob on the top; another deeply carved tapemeasure; a corozo nut, the nut from which vegetable ivory is produced; a waxer and pincushion set between two carved ends; a reel holder holding a reel of maroon-coloured silk; and a carved double-ended needlecase. (Bottom row, left to right) An acorn-shaped thimble holder (the acorn unscrews from the cup to reveal space for a thimble); a tapemeasure with a blue cotton tape; a carved double-ended pincushion with red velvet cushions; a small round, intricately carved waxer; an elaborately carved needlecase. (Centre bottom) Another small round carved waxer.

made in the Ayrshire village of Mauchline, is another common type. Most of the pieces now found are decorated with a black transfer print on a sycamore-wood base. They also date from the early nineteenth century and often feature pictures of resorts. A later type is similar, but a stuck-on photograph replaces the transfer print.

Tartan ware also came from Scotland, in the first quarter of the nineteenth century, and is said to have greatly increased in popularity when Queen Victoria built Balmoral. Originally the tartan pattern was painted on the wooden articles, but later this was replaced by the use of tartan paper glued to the wooden base.

Fernware also consists of a wooden base, decorated in the earliest pieces with real ferns, but the items most often found nowadays have applied colour decoration. This ware dates from the early twentieth century. There is also a type with red and green fern pattern.

A number of other small items in wood are painted black and decorated with coloured pictures and verses. Other pieces painted in colours came from Italy and Austria.

A less common souvenir ware – mainly pincushions and needlecases, though tapemeasures may be found – is decorated with a coloured print under glass, with a mirror on the reverse side of the article.

In addition to these souvenir wares, many needlework accessories will be found made of gold, silver, silver gilt, silver plate, mother-of-pearl, tortoiseshell (with or without piqué in gold or silver), ivory, vegetable ivory (the kernel of the corozo nut, usually darker coloured), wood, fabric, leather, horn, bone, jet, beadwork and straw-work (fine pieces of dyed, cut straw glued to a wooden base).

Beadwork sewing items. (Left-hand diagonal row, bottom to top) Two small examples of beadwork, probably from belts; a flat needlecase with black and pink beads; a red and pink fringed pincushion. (Centre diagonal row, bottom to top) An emery cushion with red corner tassels; a cylindrical needlecase; another flat needlecase with blue and pink beads; a delightful bellows-shaped needlecase covered in green silk with beadwork decoration. (Right-hand diagonal row, bottom to top) A packet of Abel Morrall's Flora Macdonald beading needles, which are especially fine for the very small beads used; a small round silk-covered pin wheel with a realistic rose decoration in beadwork; and a beadwork egg-shaped thimble holder.

NEEDLEWORK AND RELATED ACTIVITIES

The term 'needlework' covers a wide field of sewing and embroidery, but there are other related activities using the hands, and it may be helpful to the collector of the accessories used in them to describe briefly some of the main types.

Embroidery is perhaps the best-known. This is the use of a needle to stitch various designs and patterns in white or coloured threads on linen or other materials. Frequently an embroidery frame will be used to keep the work flat and evenly stretched. Other types of embroidery are carried out on holed canvas. In the past a popular form of counted thread work was the sampler; some of the most charming of these were made by little children as an exercise in various stitches.

Beadwork was a popular activity in Regency and Victorian days. Tiny beads were threaded with an extremely fine needle on to a thread or wire and then used to decorate all kinds of useful articles.

Several crafts involved knots used in a variety of ways. *Tatting*, perhaps the best-known of these today and still popular, required the use of an elliptically shaped shuttle on to which the thread was wound. This thread produced knots on a separate thread held by the other hand. *Knotting* shuttles are a larger type of the same shape. *Netting* and *macramé*, which is enjoying a revival today, also involved making knots, though only netting required special tools, with the necessary netting needle and gauges, as still used by fishermen, and a netting clamp with a hook for commencing the work.

Equipment for cordmaking and tambour work. (Left-hand group, clockwise) Four lucets for cordmaking: a wooden one; an ivory example; another wooden one with cordmaking in progress, from thread wound on to a wooden thread winder; and one in rosewood. (Right-hand group) Tambour hooks photographed with two examples of tambour work: (top) the corner of a head shawl, in very fine work on net; (below) a scrap of satin with a rose pattern; (left to right) a mother-of-pearl hook and three ivory examples.

Cordmaking was a useful art, carried out with the lucet, a now scarce and expensive tool.

When making clothing and bed linen, many long seams had to be sewn, and a valuable aid for this purpose was the pincushion clamp or hemming bird, to which the material could be pinned, with the clamp attached to the table to keep the material taut.

Tambouring was carried out with a special hook attached to a handle. The material was stretched on to an embroidery frame, and the fine hook was inserted from the top and caught the thread held underneath by the other hand, drawing it through in a series of chain stitches to outline a design.

Sewing clamps. (Top diagonal row, left to right) A green wooden box on a metal clamp; the green velvet-topped pincushion lid has a mirror inside; the box holds a yellow silk tapemeasure, and the lid is removed to show the contents of the box: an ivory needlecase, a small wooden multi-spool for thread, and an ivory thimble with a gilt band round the base. A plain wooden clamp with a reel for thread and topped with an ivory spindle and black finial; another small ivory knob on the clamp removes to reveal space for needles. A brass hemming bird, and a bronze hemming bird with a small pincushion on its back and another larger pincushion. (Far right diagonal row, left to right) An early nineteenth-century rosewood winding clamp; this would have been one of a pair. A mahogany clamp of similar date, with a reel for thread and a pincushion on top. A small rosewood clamp with a tapemeasure and a pincushion. A larger rosewood clamp with a tapemeasure and a pincushion. Another early nineteenth-century rosewood winding clamp, again one of a pair. (Centre diagonal row, top to bottom) A carved ivory clamp with a red silk rectangular pincushion. A steel netting clamp. A carved ivory winding clamp, one of a pair.

Thimble cases. (Clockwise from far left) A closed brass egg shape with a small star design; an open egg shape with a chain attached, lined in quilted green fabric with fine ric-rac braid and containing a Dorcas thimble; a purple velvet shoe with the thimble under the upper; a white china shoe with a painted bird design; a brass bird on a stand (the top body slides over to reveal the thimble space); a metal tankard with hinged lid; a rectangular pink-painted metal case with a chain attached; photographed with a First World War embroidered envelope card with the message 'Greetings from France'.

THIMBLES AND THIMBLE CASES

Thimbles have a long history and were made as a result of the need to protect the fingers when pushing an unpolished needle into tough material. Since smooth and shiny needles have been manufactured and lighter fabrics used, usually only gentle pressure from the fingertip has been required, so it has been possible to make thimbles from lighter, less durable materials, and many have been elaborately decorated. Among the collectors' items are many that are more decorative than practical, such as those of porcelain, glass and wood, although porcelain examples used to be regarded as useful in that they did not catch delicate materials.

Old porcelain thimbles have now become extremely scarce and expensive, and those most likely to be found will be fairly modern hand-painted items. Very attractive signed and hand-painted thimbles were made by Royal Worcester until 1985, and others at the Caverswall Pottery. Numerous other transfer-printed thimbles are freely available and appear in some private collections.

Silver thimbles occur in a wide variety of styles and decoration. Some have a semi-precious stone in the top or set in the lower band, or they have designs and messages engraved round the lower edge. They were made as commemorative souvenirs, for example for a jubilee or coronation, and sometimes to advertise a product. Some silver thimbles are enamelled, and these can be very attractive. Gold thimbles are also interesting to the collector and, though not always hallmarked, are desirable, but expensive.

One of the most serviceable thimbles was that which appeared under the trade name of Dorcas. It was made from a layer of steel sandwiched between two layers of silver, this type of construction making it particularly durable. Three other similar types were made, under the names of Doris, Dreema and Dura.

Other thimbles encountered include various designs in brass, nickel

Thimbles. (Far left) A Dorcas thimble with the original box in which it was sold. (To the right of this and above) A cupro-nickel thimble, made by Charles Iles, with faceted sides and the mark of three minute thimbles in a shield on the lower rim; a retailer's cardboard box. (Next diagonal row to the right, bottom to top) A Royal Worcester porcelain thimble, hand-painted and signed; early English porcelain with a hand-painted design of flowers; a silver thimble guard. (Next diagonal row, bottom to top) Two English hallmarked silver thimbles; one cloisonné thimble. (Next diagonal row, bottom to top) Three English hallmarked silver thimbles, the third one with a green stone top. (Next diagonal row, bottom to top) English hallmarked silver child's thimble; a small thimble and a larger one with alternate plain and engraved panels, both American; silver with a cornelian stone top; silver with an applied fleur-de-lis band and a cornelian stone top. (Next diagonal row, bottom to top) Silver with concentric rings of indentations; silver with a daisy pattern; silver with FELIXSTOWE round the lower rim and a cornelian stone top. (Far right) English hallmarked silver, with the maker's initials J S & S.

silver and silver plate and advertising thimbles made in brass or aluminium, sometimes with a coloured glass top, and bearing the name of a product round the lower edge. Examples made in early plastics are also fairly common.

Occasionally rarer items are found such as those made of ivory, vegetable ivory or mother-of-pearl; these mainly originated from France

Aluminium advertising, brass, bronze and steel-cored thimbles. (Top left-hand corner) A group of aluminium advertising thimbles: (left to right) with a red band, SINGER SEWING MACHINES; on red with a blue stone top, SUN TIP TEA; on blue, WHITE SEWING MACHINES; on red, CRAWFORD'S BISCUITS, the lettering the opposite way up to the usual. (Back group of eight to the right) Brass thimbles: (from the left) one with a patterned lower band; one advertising BARBOUR'S LINEN THREAD; one with HER MAJESTY'S THIMBLE, ENGLAND on the lower border; one advertising HUDSON'S SOAP; one with a patterned lower border; two others with different patterns; and one advertising SKINNER & ROOK. Silver-coloured thimbles: (front left to right) steel-cored, marked P A T 6; two Dorcas, diamond-patterned; two Dreema, one above the other; a Dorcas; a thimble with worn silver plating and the Charles Horner mark; an early bronze example; Dreema, with the initials HG&S (Henry Griffiths & Sons); two more Dreema of different designs.

Wooden thimble holders. (Far left) A yew-wood acorn shape. (Next diagonal row, bottom to top) A boxwood bell shape; an acorn shape with a vegetable-ivory nut in a carved wooden cup; a fruitwood barrel. (Next diagonal pair, bottom to top) A rosewood egg-cup with a vegetable-ivory egg (the egg removes to reveal the thimble space); an ebony egg-cup with applied ivory brass-studded strips, with an ivory egg. (Next diagonal pair, bottom to top) A lignum-vitae egg and cup; a rosewood urn shape on a stand. (Far right pair, left to right) A boxwood churn shape; and a carved and pierced coquilla-nut egg shape.

and are known as *Palais Royal*. Another rare type is tortoiseshell decorated with gold or silver inlay or piqué.

Tailors' thimbles are open at the top, as tailors customarily used the side of the thimble.

A wide range of more modern thimbles can now be found in metal and china, either commemorative or with varied decoration.

'Hunt the thimble' used to be a popular childhood game. One can speculate that it may have originated when a mother, having mislaid her precious and indispensable sewing aid, enlisted the help of her children to find it.

Thimble cases are practical in more ways than one, and there is seemingly no end to the variety and ingenuity displayed in making these highly collectable items. They appear in all the souvenir wares, carved and turned wood, including bog-oak, ivory and vegetable ivory, tortoiseshell and mother-of-pearl. These last are often egg-shaped or in the shape of a miniature knife box and, though desirable, are now very scarce.

Examples shaped like an acorn or a beehive, the top unscrewing to reveal the space for a thimble, are fairly common, and wood and vegetable ivory appear as an egg in an egg-cup.

Leather cases in the shape of a thimble are found, and also some very attractive items with decorated beadwork. Another charming variety is the small shoe, in velvet, china or glass, containing the thimble; others were hand-made in fabric.

Thimble cases also sometimes incorporate some other essential tool; for example, a needlecase or a thimble and a finger guard nestle closely together in the same case. The finger guard was to protect the finger of the hand not using the needle, preventing the needle from being stuck into the finger supporting the fabric.

NEEDLECASES

In the early days of needlework needles were scarce and expensive, and because they were so small and easily mislaid a variety of containers was devised to keep them in. Some were made in precious metals, but these are not often found now. China and glass examples are fairly rare but do occasionally turn up. Most commonly they were in cylindrical shapes.

The more usual form is that of a needlebook: leaves of flannel, folded between two covers of harder material, and tied at the front with silk ribbon. These were made in all the souvenir wares, mother-of-pearl, carved or decorated ivory, painted wood, paper and embroidered card known as Bristol board.

Another fairly common type is an umbrella or parasol shape, mostly in wood, ivory or bone. Sometimes these have a tiny viewer, with magnified photographs of a popular resort, in the handle; this is known as a 'Stanhope'.

There is a great variety of wooden needlecases: turned and carved in many shapes and designs such as animals; or continental ones often in two coloured woods, and perhaps carved to resemble an ear of corn. There are many plain cylindrical shapes, others like a rolling pin, and yet another upright variety with a marked metal top, indicating compartments for different-sized needles.

The more specially sought-after varieties include wood or ivory items shaped like a pea-pod, beadwork and the very interesting Avery needlecases. These were made mostly in brass (although an early plastic item, a cradle, has been seen) by the Redditch needle-making firm of Avery. They come in a fascinating variety of ingenious shapes; for example barrows, fans, shells, insects, a picture on an easel, a basket, a

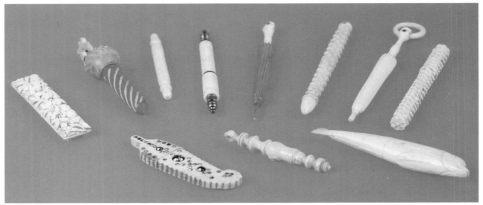

Needlecases in ivory and bone. (Top row, left to right) A Dieppe floral carved rectangular shape; an elaborate parasol shape with a vegetable-ivory top and red-dyed and cream bone spiral below; a small cylindrical ivory case; a bone rolling-pin shape with brass finials; a red-dyed bone parasol with the top shaped like a hand; a basket-weave carved cylinder in ivory with a Stanhope in the top, the view no longer visible; an ivory parasol shape with a ring on the top of the handle and a Stanhope with views of Le Havre; another ivory basket-weave carved cylindrical shape with floral carved ends. (Bottom row, left to right) A bone feather shape inlaid with large and small steel studs; a small bobbin-turned bone; and a bone mackerel shape.

cottage or a walnut on a leaf. The metal container held packets of needles. The name of Avery is always stamped on, and some are marked with the Victorian registration mark, which enables them to be accurately dated. These cases are now rather scarce and have become expensive as they are in great demand.

Another type made by Avery and other manufacturers is a slim rectangular box with a hinged top. Near the bottom is a small lever that can be moved to a number representing a size of needle. With the lid open, the movement pushes up a metal container with a packet of needles of that size. 'Mitrailleuse' (a French word for a machine-gun) is the name for a cylindrical metal container, the movable top exposing compartments for different-sized needles.

Needlecases and boxes in wood, tortoiseshell and card. (Far left, bottom to top) A burr-walnut box with sloping front; a gold-decorated imitation-leather-covered card box with a sloping-fronted lid, inscribed with the word NEEDLES; *both these are for packets of needles. (Next diagonal row, bottom to top) A rare olive-wood souvenir pea-pod shape, with an indecipherable place-name; two coquilla-nut shapes, the first a fish; a box-wood clog. (Lying flat) A rectangular needlebook with a carved motif on the cover, lined in pale blue silk. (Next diagonal row, bottom to top) A brass-studded boot shape, the lower part rosewood and the upper boxwood; a rectangular box, a souvenir of Lausanne with a coloured print on the underside; a fruitwood crocodile; a Tyrolean carved fish shape; a double-ended container, the centre boxwood and the ends rosewood; an oval striped wooden case with ivory oval decoration; an upright rosewood container with a circular brass top marked with needle sizes, containing steel sewing-machine needles and a curious steel hooked tool. (Far right, from bottom) A tortoiseshell box shaped like a knife box, to hold packets of needles; a turned rosewood turret-shaped container with a wind-out flannel strip on which to store needles. Photographed with a hand-stitched miniature shirt, perfect in every detail.*

Wooden needlecases. (Top row, left to right) A carved olive-wood parasol shape; a boxwood parasol with a bone handle; a rosewood candle holder with a bone candle; a fine continental carved figure on a stand; another stand topped with a carved marmot; a fine carved Flemish figure. (Bottom row, left to right) A parasol in plain dark wood with an ivory handle and band; a parasol in box-wood with a rosewood ring and ferrule and bone handle; an olive-wood souvenir parasol from Menton, with a cream plastic handle; a carved wooden parasol topped with a carved hand holding a Stanhope with views of Brighton; a double-ended carved continental wooden bodkin holder with leaves and grapes; another with carved edelweiss decoration. Photographed with a sample piece of genuine Madeira broderie anglaise or eyelet work, with its original label.

A folding cardboard needle box. The lid, which holds the sides upright, is raised to show the inside. The box is lined in pale pink silk, and there is a packet of needles under each ribbon, with four more round the central small box, which holds a thimble.

Brass and other metals were used for embossed cylindrical containers, some of which are larger to hold bodkins for threading ribbon or elastic; and there are some elaborately decorated articles in book form.

Paper and card needlebooks and boxes are among the more charming collectors' items, though because of their fragile nature not many have survived. There are paper caskets of many shapes; needlebooks made from embroidered, punched-card Bristol board, this work being a popular craft in Victorian times; and little boxes the size of a packet of needles, decorated on top with one of the attractive prints made by George Baxter or one of his licensees. These prints were made in sheets

Five novelty Avery needlecases. (Top row, left to right) A wheelbarrow; a weight; a well; a hat box. (Centre) A butterfly. Packets of needles are held in clips inside the models.

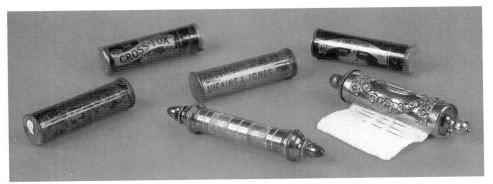

Metal needlecases. (Back row, left to right) A black mitrailleuse case, advertising Cross-Fox; another, red, advertising the Regent Street store Dickins & Jones; a green one, advertising Alfred Shrimpton & Sons. (Bottom row, left to right) A brown mitrailleuse, advertising W. Woodfield & Sons of Redditch; a double-ended brass bodkin case; and a silver metal container with a wind-out flannel strip in which to insert needles.

of the required size and came to be known as needleprints. Perhaps the most charming paper caskets are those made to look like a box, the top and sides decorated with coloured pictures. When the lid is lifted the sides fall separately, to reveal a delightful silk-lined interior, each of the sides holding a packet of needles under a ribbon, and in the centre a much smaller square box with a removable lid and containing a thimble.

Avery brass needlecases. (Top row, left to right) 'The Royal Avery', a rectangular purse shape, with packet holders that slide out of the container; a four-packet folding container in its original box, 'The Beatrice'; a similar folding type for six packets, also 'The Beatrice'; an Avery basket (the lift-up lids have clips to hold packets of needles, and the base of the basket is marked AVERY & SON, REDDITCH and has the Victorian registration mark). (Bottom row, left to right) A 'Quadruple Golden Casket' (the hinged lid lifts and the small knob on the front slides to push up containers for different sizes of needles); a square type with a hinged lid for two packets of needles, 'The Louise'; a rectangular purse shape, also 'The Louise' (this is a commemorative for the marriage of Princess Louise in 1871); a lift-up bee on a leaf, the needle packets fitting inside.

Novelty pincushions. (Back row, left to right) A delightful hand-embroidered cottage; a red, white and blue patchwork jockey cap; a metal shoe with a roller-skate attached; a small brass bird with a pincushion on its back; a carved ivory pin wheel with a red silk cushion. (Centre row, left to right) A metal shoe; a rosewood cooking-pot shape with a metal and ivory handle; a rosewood urn on a stand with a red velvet cushion; a small wooden pin wheel with an engraved plate attached. (Bottom row, left to right) A hallmarked silver pig; a small painted ivory pin wheel inscribed 'Friendship'; a brightly coloured miniature patchwork pin wheel.

PINCUSHIONS AND EMERY CUSHIONS

Pincushions and emery cushions introduce us to the wealth of skill and ingenuity exercised by Victorian and Edwardian needlewomen. It would be impossible to catalogue every variation, for one is always coming across something new. How often one longs to know whose fingers sewed the tiny stitches that made the minute patchwork pincushions or threaded the tiny beads with extremely fine needles to form the intricate designs! Scraps of left-over fabric, stuffed with bran or sheep's wool to prevent the pins from rusting, were fashioned into ever more imaginative shapes, such as flowers, stars, baskets and shoes. Miniature jockey caps are also found occasionally.

The talented amateur artists of the period had scope to demonstrate their skill in pin wheels, with a picture painted on silk or fine fabric. The wheel was made from two fabric-covered circles of card joined together, the pins being stuck round the outside between the layers. Knitting and crochet were also used to cover small pin balls, which could be suspended from the waist.

Manufacturers produced pincushions in all the usual souvenir wares, often round, but also shaped like hearts, diamonds and clubs. Ivory and mother-of-pearl were popular, two flat circles or other shapes enclosing a narrow pincushion. More unusual were tiny ivory bellows, barrows, butterflies and other shapes.

Natural shells of many types were pressed into use for pincushions and make an attractive addition to a collection, as do those in the form

A varied collection of pincushions. (Top left) A large fabric-covered cushion advertising Dewhurst's Sylko Machine Twist, with the trademark of three shells, and the thickness of thread number 40. (Next diagonal row, bottom to top) A china pear with leaf and green velvet cushion; a double-ended ivory barrel shape on feet with green velvet cushions and carrying handle; a large realistic wooden shoe. (Next diagonal row, bottom to top) A shell-covered 'Souvenir de Trouville'; a carved ivory pin wheel; a rosewood stand topped with a velvet cushion; a modern square hand-embroidered needlepoint cushion with a rose design, in the style of older examples. (Far right pair, bottom to top) A shell-covered heart shape with a circular brass central decoration; and an ebony combined pincushion and waxer.

Layette pincushions. (Left to right) A fabric-covered flower-shaped cushion with a cotton fringe and the message 'Welcome sweet innocent', a design of leaves, stems and three ostrich feathers in pins. A satin-covered rectangular cushion with a silk fringe, a design of vases of flowers and the message 'Lord sanctify this solemn hour, thy spirit on this infant pour, fulfil thy promise to the child, may it in Christ be reconcil'd, Feb'y 1846, Welcome little stranger', all depicted in pins.

of china animals or pieces of fruit.

Wood and metal are used in many ways, the former making a turned stand topped by a velvet pincushion or a carved bog-oak kitchen utensil, such as a cauldron or saucepan. Birds and animals in base metal are found in variety, together with the much sought-after brass pigs.

Silver pincushions are in the luxury class and are now scarce and expensive. English hallmarked items, mostly dating from the early twentieth century, are usually animals or birds, but fish, shoes or even

A collection of pincushions. (Clockwise from left) A tiny square patchwork example with very small pins inserted in regular patterns; a round dark red leather-covered cushion with a gold design; an octagonal shell-decorated cushion with a picture of the Crystal Palace on the back; a circular silk-covered pin wheel with a hand-painted coastal scene finished with a silk ribbon; a white silk-covered playing card with red-painted diamonds, the pins inserted round the sides; a brown circular silk cushion with divisions marked in gold thread and finished with a brown and gold ribbon. (Centre) A purple velvet cushion on plain gilded wood.

a tiny cradle may be found. Continental silver items, such as baskets, are delightful and delicately made.

Another now scarce item, but one well worth searching for, is a pin poppet. These mostly date from the late eighteenth century and appear in a variety of shapes, perhaps a pear, an acorn or a pine-cone. The top unscrews to reveal a tiny silk pincushion, to hold much smaller pins than those now generally in use.

Two larger types of pincushion may also interest the collector: the layette, and those given by sailors and soldiers to their girlfriends as love tokens. The former was a popular gift to an expectant mother and was usually made in pillow or flower shapes, with a design in flowers and a welcome message pricked out in pins. The sailors' and soldiers' cushions were very elaborate, often heart-shaped, incorporating decorative glass-headed pins, woven silk messages and pictures, together

A collection of metal pincushions. (Back row, left to right) A small black pug dog with a red velvet cushion; a silver metal bird with a blue velvet cushion on its back; a silver metal shoe with a picture of the Woolworth Building in New York on the tongue and the cushion behind it; a donkey; a brass pig with a green velvet cushion. (Centre) A small brass hexagonal box with a green velvet cushion in the lid.

A large heart-shaped, mainly green-coloured soldier's pincushion. Such cushions were made as gifts for family or friends. The cushion is fabric-covered and decorated with a printed regimental name and badge, surrounded with circles of beads edged with pins stuck through beads, together with a woven silk message and flags on silk attached at the top corners.

with the name of the man's regiment or ship.

Pincushion-topped boxes are fairly common. Many were lead-weighted and could be used to anchor material while sewing. Many of these date from Regency times, while some later boxes had lift-off or sliding lids that reveal a compartment for small sewing items or trinkets.

Another type of cushion, though not for pins, is the emery cushion. These come in many styles and materials, often as a matching piece in a fitted workbox. The cushion is filled with emery powder, which makes it feel heavier, and a needle could be pushed in and out to remove rust. One type often met is a small fabric or knitted strawberry, decorated with small yellow beads to add realism.

A collection of novelty pincushions. (Clockwise from far left bottom) A small bone basket with a brass handle and containing a green silk cushion; a black wooden cauldron with a handle and containing a red velvet cushion; a shell with a blue silk cushion; a china apple with its leaf and a velvet pincushion; a small straw-work basket; and a musical instrument with the cushion in the lower part.

23

TAPEMEASURES

The tapemeasure is a valuable aid to needlework and was often used by the lady of the house to check the measurement of materials that she bought from a travelling salesman calling at her door. Each household had a wooden yardstick from which to mark the measure in the days before tapemeasures were printed.

Early measures, up to about the middle of the nineteenth century, were marked in nails, a measurement of $2^{1}/_{4}$ inches (5.7 cm); later the normal inch (2.5 cm) was used. There are many designs, and tapemeasures could form a collection on their own. The earliest ones were wound into the container by a handle, the measure itself usually being

Novelty metal tapemeasures, mostly wind-in. (Back row, left to right) A thimble shape containing the tape, with a small Middle Eastern figure sitting sewing on the top; an owl with a top hat; an owl with a rust-coloured breast, on a stand; another similar, with a pale blue breast; a clock with a recoil spring tape. (Centre row, left to right) A copper-coloured ship's wheel; a bird standing on its own feet; another owl; a smoothing iron with an agate stone in the handle; a copper-coloured coffee grinder. (Bottom three, left to right) A brass pig; an elegant brass coffee pot; and a copper coffee pot with a brass lid.

Tapemeasures of wood, nut and fabric, all wind-in. (Left to right) Coquilla-nut; yew-wood with a pink tape marked in nails; another coquilla-nut example; a rosewood urn shape; a boxwood urn shape; a small round bun shape; a combined needlecase and tapemeasure in boxwood, with a Stanhope in the winding handle, having views of Edinburgh; a rosewood barrel shape with an ivory winding handle; one in lignum-vitae with an ivory winding handle. (Front) A hand-painted flower-decorated silk ribbon tape on metal rollers.

made of silk ribbon. These were followed by the use of a spring mechanism.

As with other tools, tapemeasures were made in a great variety of materials and shapes. Wind-in examples come in silver, sometimes with a ring attached to hang on a chatelaine chain. Shells were used. Metal appeared as animals, birds, household objects such as clocks and coffee grinders, smoothing irons, buildings, lamps, a coronation coach, a sewing machine and other novelties. Ivory, vegetable ivory, mother-of-pearl and wood were also frequently used.

Tapemeasures with a spring mechanism come in great variety: china dolls or animals, metal novelties advertising items, or a round shape with a picture in the top. Finally, there are many in early plastic materials, such as baskets of fruit and flowers, ships, heads, dice, hats and pieces of fruit, etc.

Novelty tapemeasures. (Far left diagonal pair, bottom to top) A china crinoline doll, German; a plastic windmill. (Next diagonal row, bottom to top) A plastic pear; the head of King Edward VIII; and a ship. (Next diagonal row, bottom to top) A circular brass tape advertising Ashworth's sewing cotton; circular silver metal with King Edward VII and Queen Alexandra in their youth as Prince and Princess of Wales; a plastic chess table. (Far right diagonal row, bottom to top) A plastic purse; a plastic clock; and a plastic box with a seated Chinaman. All these have a recoil spring mechanism.

A very attractive metal tapemeasure shaped like an oil table lamp, with an insect on the end of the wind-in tape.

A collection of novelty tapemeasures. (Top row, left to right) A plastic ship; china horseshoes with a gold pig topping a circular tape; a shell; a metal basket of flowers; a green plastic gondola. (Middle row, left to right) A plastic boater hat with a coat of arms on the top; a plastic strawberry; a metal souvenir of the Wolverhampton Exhibition of 1902. (Bottom centre) A plastic fish. All except the shell have recoil spring mechanisms to wind in the tapes.

THREAD HOLDERS, WINDERS, WAXERS AND REEL STANDS

Many workboxes during the early nineteenth century were fitted with cotton barrels to hold thread. The barrel had a spindle inside and a hole in the side, from which the thread could be drawn. They were made in ivory and wood, including Tunbridge ware. The barrels were succeeded by reel holders, mostly with a carved mother-of-pearl top and bone base, joined by a slim hollow metal rod, one end fitting inside the other. Carved ivory reels were also made, but they are not very common. Wooden cotton reels did not make their appearance until 1820–30, and these were in due course replaced by plastic ones in 1966.

A large variety of reel boxes was made in all the souvenir wares and plain polished wood. These boxes have pegs inside to hold the reels and holes in the sides, through which the thread can emerge; they often have a label inside the lid advertising Clark's Anchor cotton. Some other manufacturers' labels are also found.

In the past embroidery silks were very soft and loose-fibred, so the skeins were wound on to thread winders to prevent the silk from

Silk winders. (Far left vertical row) Three different wooden shapes, one with an inlaid mother-of-pearl disc. (Next vertical row, bottom to top) Bone dyed red; a circular ivory shape; a gold-decorated orange-coloured card wound with silk; a bone shape with black thread; a rare square yellow glass example. (Centre group of four, bottom to top) A wooden pokerwork-decorated flower shape; an ivory star; an ivory Maltese cross shape; and a cream plastic multi-holder, inscribed 'School of Embroidery, Clive Chambers, Windsor Place, Cardiff', photographed with a skein of blue Filoselle silk of the type which would have been wound on to silk winders. (Far right, bottom to top) A French printed card shape, with the wording CARTE TRAMWAY, *a picture of a horse-drawn tram, and the initials JP; a wooden star; and a wooden teddy bear.*

Right: A stained wood reel stand with one gallery, pegs for twelve reels of thread, and topped with a velvet pincushion. The wooden reels of Sylko are much later than the stand.

becoming tangled. There are many different shapes, made in a variety of materials, including mother-of-pearl, ivory, bone, wood (in the souvenir wares), plastic and even glass.

The thread used for sewing was not originally mercerised and smooth, and so the cotton was drawn across a thread waxer to make it slide easily through the material and to strengthen it. Beeswax or candle wax was used; it was also

Below: A collection of reel stands. (Clockwise from the left) A pierced brass stand, with a revolving gallery for six reels of thread; a fine nineteenth-century rosewood stand with two revolving galleries and holders for three thimbles, topped with a pincushion (these two stands carry later wooden reels of Sylko); another fine-quality nineteenth-century stand with one revolving gallery carrying older reels of thread and topped with its original brown velvet pincushion; another rosewood stand with one revolving gallery, topped with a pincushion; a smaller stand with a single gallery, space for a thimble and topped with a brown velvet pincushion; a small wooden stand with a spiral-twist boxwood spindle. (Centre) A rare rosewood cornucopia stand with six bone pegs for reels and a velvet pincushion. Originally the small turned part on the left of this stand would have held a tapemeasure, but this is missing.

27

Cotton boxes, a cotton barrel and reels. (Top row, left to right) Open, a painted wooden spherical holder with a hole in the top and inside a label 'Clark & Co's Anchor sewing cotton, Clark & Co's extra quality', and the number 10 denoting thickness of thread; a rosewood cotton box with holes in the side for the thread to emerge and a very small velvet pincushion on the top. (Bottom row, left to right) A wooden reel with a painted top and the original thread, I. P. Clark's Patent Excelsior thread 26, number 5; a wooden cotton barrel with its spindle and a hole in the side; a smaller version of the reel of I. P. Clark's thread, number 16; and a wooden black-painted box with retailer's label in the lid and compartments inside to hold reels of thread, painted with lilies of the valley and a message.

possible to buy small cakes of wax wrapped in foil, which could then be fixed between two circles of carved mother-of-pearl, ivory, bone or wood. Waxers are quite often found combined with tapemeasures or pincushions.

In order to keep reels of cotton at hand and ready to use, reel stands were employed. They were made of metal or turned wood on a circular base with revolving or fixed galleries and had pegs on which to place the reels. The stand was usually topped with a pincushion, and some had a wooden acorn shape to hold a thimble. The earlier ones are small and dainty, while many of the later ones are heavy and more clumsy. Especially large ones were used in haberdashery shops.

Scissors. (Back row, left to right) Steel buttonhole scissors; a larger pair with decorative handles; a leather-covered case lined in red satin, with matching pairs of steel scissors; a silver-handled pair; a folding pair with tortoiseshell handles; a decorative brass-handled pair; and a large plain steel pair. (Centre, left to right) Miniature brass-handled scissors and a silver metal stork design. (Bottom row, left to right) Polished steel; a delicate fine-bladed pair; another pair of buttonhole scissors of a different type.

SCISSORS

Scissors, an essential tool of the needlewoman, were made in a great variety of shapes, sizes and materials, including silver gilt, silver, steel and even ivory. Many have beautifully decorated handles, mother-of-pearl and tortoiseshell occasionally being used. Those made in the shape of a crane or stork are popular, and another interesting type of collectors' item is a matching set in a case. One early form of scissors is made like a miniature pair of sheep shears. Folding scissors are fairly common, some simply folding so that the sharp part of the blades is not enclosed, and others folding completely, revealing only the ivory or tortoiseshell handles. Scissors of a special type with a section cut out of the blade for cutting buttonholes are fairly common, but occasionally rarer types turn up, such as a long-bladed pair, with inches and measurements marked on the blade.

MISCELLANEOUS ACCESSORIES

Sewing clamps or *hemming birds* are much sought after and have become extremely rare and expensive. They are made mainly in brass or bronze. A metal clamp to fix to the table is topped by a bird whose beak opens when the tail is depressed. The closed beak then holds the material firm while sewing proceeds. Other shapes, such as a dolphin, a butterfly or a fish, were also made. One or two pincushions are usually incorporated, and sometimes a container for needles.

Winding clamps, usually made in ivory, bone or wood, were supplied in pairs. The clamps had revolving cages or reels on top, over which the skein of thread was placed to be wound into a ball (which could be placed in the cup-shaped piece on top of the cage if necessary) or on to a thread winder.

Pincushion clamps were simply a pincushion on top of a clamp and were used, in a similar way to hemming birds, to anchor the material with pins.

Netting clamps had a metal hook attached to a clamp and were used to commence netting.

Sometimes several of these clamps will be found in combination, and a tapemeasure, too, may be included.

Tambour hook and spool-knave. The tambour hook was usually made of ivory or mother-of-pearl, and the ivory handle concealed a metal hook,

A collection of wooden sewing items. (Top left pair, left to right) A wooden pin poppet (the pointed top removes to reveal a very small pincushion in the base); a rosewood turret-shaped container with a tapemeasure in the top and a pincushion in the base. (The two items below these, left to right) A boxwood workbox vinaigrette with holes in the lid (the box could hold lavender flowers or a sponge soaked in aromatic vinegar); a rosewood carved double-ended waxer. (Next two to the right, bottom to top) A carved coquilla-nut workbox vinaigrette; a green-painted pine-cone-shaped pin poppet. (Next row, bottom to top) A rosewood Tunbridge ware pin poppet with mosaic-decorated top and base; a fruitwood plain cone-shaped pin poppet, open, showing the pincushion; a slim wooden workbox vinaigrette inlaid with polished steel. (Far right row, bottom to top) A small circular rosewood waxer; a shaped wooden inch measure (marked with three inches); a rosewood bottle-shaped vinaigrette with pierced ivory top. Photographed with a skein of apricot-coloured Filoselle silk.

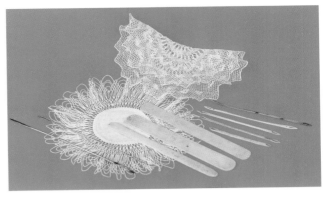

Netting tools photographed with two doyleys made from netting. (Left to right) Two thin metal netting needles; three bone netting gauges in different widths to set the size of the netted holes; five small bone netting needles.

which by means of a screw could be fitted into position for working. The spool-knave was used in conjunction with this tool; it consists of a ring to slip over the wrist, and from this is suspended a removable, revolving rod between two metal stays. The ball or reel of thread is inserted on to the metal rod and thus runs freely while work is in progress.

Tatting and knotting shuttles. These shuttles are larger and smaller sizes of the same shape and can be very decorative. Most of those found today are in carved ivory, plain ivory, bone, mother-of-pearl, tortoiseshell and also metal and plastics. Some of the metal examples have a hook attached. This is necessary for the work, but usually a separate tool is preferred. A chain with a small hook attached, joined to a ring to slip on the finger, is sometimes found.

Hand coolers. These are egg-shaped pieces of stone that were used to keep the hands fresh when handling fine fabrics.

Workbox vinaigrettes and powder sprinklers. The vinaigrette is a small box, usually wood or ivory. The top unscrews to reveal a small perforated lid to an inner container, in which could be placed lavender flowers or wadding soaked in aromatic vinegars. Powder sprinklers were used to keep the hands dry and fresh while working.

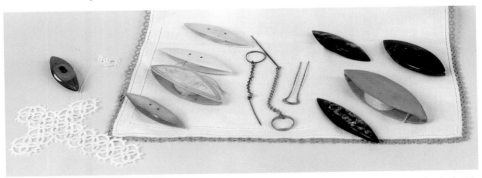

Equipment for tatting. (Far left, bottom to top) A white tatted bookmark in the form of a cross; a plastic shuttle wound with thread with work commenced. (Next diagonal row to the right, bottom to top) A plain mother-of-pearl shuttle; a larger decorated mother-of-pearl knotting shuttle; and two ivory shuttles. (Centre) Three brass tatting pins. (Far right group of four, bottom to top) A shuttle made in papier-mâché inlaid with abalone shell; a large wooden shuttle; and two tortoiseshell examples. All photographed on a handkerchief edged with blue tatting.

31

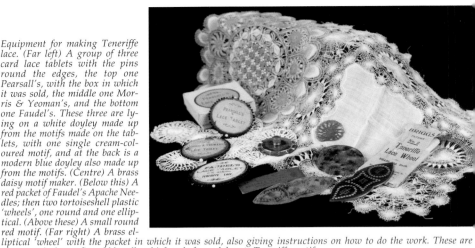

Equipment for making Teneriffe lace. (Far left) A group of three card lace tablets with the pins round the edges, the top one Pearsall's, with the box in which it was sold, the middle one Morris & Yeoman's, and the bottom one Faudel's. These three are lying on a white doyley made up from the motifs made on the tablets, with one single cream-coloured motif, and at the back is a modern blue doyley also made up from the motifs. (Centre) A brass daisy motif maker. (Below this) A red packet of Faudel's Apache Needles; then two tortoiseshell plastic 'wheels', one round and one elliptical. (Above these) A small round red motif. (Far right) A brass elliptical 'wheel' with the packet in which it was sold, also giving instructions on how to do the work. These are photographed on a fine old handkerchief made from elaborate Teneriffe motifs.

Sewing or nanny brooches. Strictly these come under the heading of jewellery, but they are of interest to the collector of needlework tools; they date from Edwardian times. The brooch has a thicker than usual bar, often with a round or diamond-shaped goldstone set in the centre. One end of the bar unscrews to reveal a hollow metal tube containing a needle and pins, with black and white cotton wound round the tube. Children's nurses wore the brooch, probably at the high neck of the blouse, and should one of their small charges tear a garment or lose a button an immediate repair could be carried out.

Netting needles and gauges. These were usually made in wood or bone. The needle is a flat tool with an open forked shape at one or both ends. The gauges are flat pieces of different widths used to fix the size of the holes in the netting.

Lucets. These were used for making cords for fastenings or trimmings and were made in mother-of-pearl, ivory, bone or wood.

Teneriffe lace wheels and tablets. These were made in metal, plastic and paper, in circular or elliptical shapes, and were used to make motifs from thread wound round pins inserted in the holes or edge of the tool. The motifs were subsequently joined together to make larger doyleys. A similar tool is the circular daisy maker, with pegs that can be wound out to extend round the edge and used in the same manner as the lace wheel.

Stilettos. These were used mainly for *broderie anglaise* or eyelet embroidery,

Stilettos photographed on a small piece of broderie anglaise or eyelet work of the type for which they were used. (Clockwise from far left centre) Carved ivory-handled steel tool; small plain steel; wooden handle; two with mother-of-pearl handles; another wooden handle; ivory handle; decorated silver handle; ivory stiletto; small stiletto with silver handle, another ivory; bright-cut steel with elaborate gilt handle; bright-cut steel with brass handle; ivory handle; Indian spotted silver in its sheath.

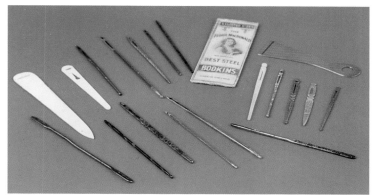

Bodkins and ribbon threaders. (Top row, left to right) Two ribbon threaders, the first cream-coloured plastic, and the second smaller and of white plastic; then five bodkins: brass; steel with brass eye and knob; silver-coloured metal; two plain steel; a packet of Flora Macdonald bodkins; a flat silver ribbon threader. (Below this, left to right) Five bodkins: mother-of-pearl; pinchbeck; gilt metal; silver metal; another gilt. (Bottom row, left to right) Double-eyed steel; blue-black steel with alternating silver metal spirals; an inscribed rare commemorative bodkin with the wording 'The beloved Queen' and, underneath, 'Victoria died Jan. 22 1901', with a cross at either end of each inscription; plain steel; steel with brass eye and knob; and plain steel.

to make holes in the fabric that were subsequently overcast. They are mostly made from steel with handles of silver or other metals, mother-of-pearl, ivory or bone. Some more delicate ones were made completely from mother-of-pearl or ivory.

Bodkins and ribbon threaders. These were for threading ribbon, tape or elastic through a casing in fabric or eyelet holes. They were made in a variety of types, mostly slim and narrow; the majority were metal, some being decorated and other rarer ones having a commemorative message and date engraved on them. Some ribbon threaders are shaped differently, made in flat metal with a slit in a triangular base.

Needle threaders. These are for threading very small-eyed needles with fine thread. Several different devices were made. One early type has a handle with the metal threading part on the top. Another type, usually in brass, has a spring mechanism, and, lastly, there is a well-known type made of a loop of very fine wire.

Although not strictly needlework, there is a wide and interesting variety of collectable items associated with knitting.

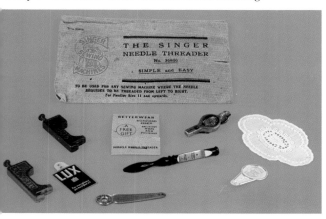

Needle threaders. (Back centre) A Singer needle threader in its original packaging. (Far left to right) Two patent spring-loaded types; a Lux advertising example with fine wire threader; a patent brass threader; a Betterwear free-gift threader; a patent threader in an ebony handle; a patent brass type; the well-known fine wire type.

33

Knitting-needle gauges and a row counter. (Back row, left to right) A bell shape made by Beehive; a drum shape with pictures of children round the sides, advertising Viyella; just below this, an expanding finger-ring row counter; a beehive shape made by Beehive. (Centre row, left to right) A painted rectangular knitting-needle and hemming gauge, advertising Rinso; a grey-painted bell shape made by Aero; a brass heart-shaped knitting-needle and wire gauge, 'The Fairfax'. (Bottom pair, left to right) A circular hook, pin and wire gauge, 'The Coronet'; and a triangular knitting-needle gauge, 'The Embassy'.

Knitting needles. These are in pairs with knobs on the ends, or in sets of four pointed at both ends. The latter were used for circular knitting such as socks or gloves. Knitting needles were made in bone, imitation tortoiseshell and some early plastics. Sets of fine steel ones could be used to make knitted lace.

Knitting-needle guards. These are employed to prevent the stitches of knitting done on sets of four needles, pointed at both ends, from slipping off the needles. They are in pairs in a variety of shapes and materials and are joined by a piece of elastic that stretches the length of the needles.

Knitting-needle gauges. These are for checking the size of unmarked knitting needles. They are in many different shapes, mostly in metal but sometimes early plastics, and have holes marked with the sizes. Many feature the name of the maker.

Knitting-needle holders. Many different sorts of cylindrical holders were made to keep the needles. Some were made in wooden souvenir wares such as Mauchline ware; one of this type has a slit in the side through which the knitting could extend. Others were made in carved or painted wood, and others in metal with a revolving top that covered a hole through which the needles could be extracted. This type had the name of the maker on the side.

Knitting frames and knitting tubes. Peg knitting frames were used to make circular pieces of knitting, for purses, caps, scarves and bags. They were made in polished wood in several sizes. The knitting tube, or 'nancy', is a similar though much smaller device for making cords. It is a hollow wooden or ivory tube with pins in the top, used in the same way as a frame. This idea is familiar to many children, who later used a simple wooden cotton reel with nails in the top.

Wool winders. Knitting wool or yarns were originally supplied in skeins and had to be

Pegged knitting devices. (Top centre) A round wooden pegged frame for knitting largish items such as caps, purses or scarves, showing the method of working. (Bottom left) A wooden knitting tube, or 'nancy', a smaller device, comprising a hollow tube with pins in the top for making fine cords. (Far right) A more elaborate type of knitting nancy made in boxwood, used for the same purpose as the previous example.

Knitting sheaths. (Top row, bottom to top) Three sheaths in turned wood of different designs; a Yorkshire goose-wing type in wood; a well-worn wooden hand-carved example, dated 1775, with a slanting groove to slip over the apron; and a further turned wooden one. (Bottom row, bottom to top) A fine-quality example with decorative wood inlay and an inlaid bone diamond, also with a groove and a framed message (these devices were often used in sheaths made as love tokens); an elaborate carved wooden sheath with chain and clew- or ball-holder, all carved from a single piece of wood.

wound into a ball ready for use. For this purpose several mainly wooden devices were used. There were floor-standing frames with two revolving cages attached to the top and bottom, table-standing models and a type that had extending arms and could be clamped to a table.

Wool-ball holders. These were round hollow wooden balls that came apart in the middle, with a hole in the top and a hanging cord attached. They were made mainly in decorated wood – some in tartan ware, Mauchline ware or fernware, and others black-painted with coloured decoration. Later versions were made in plastic materials such as Bakelite. Smaller versions with all-over coloured decoration were probably used for balls of crochet cotton. Another wool-ball holder is an open turned wooden bowl with a flat base, to hold the ball and keep it from unravelling on the floor.

Knitting sheaths. Early knitting needles were made without knobs on the ends, and a special tool, known as a sheath, was made to support one needle in the work. It was tucked under the arm or hooked on to the waistband of a skirt or apron to enable the knitter to work more quickly. Many people augmented their low incomes by knitting while they minded sheep or travelled by horse and cart. The sheaths are usually made of wood and have a hole in the top to take one end of the needle. There is a wide variety of shapes, mostly characteristic of a particular area. Many were hand-carved as love tokens, and some were bobbin-turned.

A wooden wool winder, a table model with adjustable expanding arms on which to place a skein of wool for winding into a ball.

Knitting-wool holders. (Top row, left to right) A wooden black-painted spherical holder with a hole in the top for the yarn to emerge and a carrying cord; a fine-quality polished wood cage to stand on the table or floor; another round wool-ball holder in Mauchline ware with a print of Hastings Castle. (Bottom pair) A small lignum-vitae bowl with a flat base; and a plain wooden holder on which to wind wool, featuring the cat Felix, who usually 'kept on walking'.

Knitting equipment. (Left-hand group, from bottom to top). A pair of large wooden knobbed needles; a pair of ivory guards; a white plastic stitch holder; a pair of black knitting-needle guards shaped like animal hooves; two paper packets of sets of four steel needles (the last few items photographed on a fine knitted lace doyley; and a metal mitrailleuse case, 'The Crescent Case of Best Knitting Pins, Redditch'. (Right-hand group, from left to right) A fine polished wooden container with acorn-shaped ends; a plain wooden container for

a set of double-ended needles, size 10, 'The Universal'; a pair of plastic knitting needles, blue with black knobs; a mitrailleuse knitting-needle holder; a set of four imitation-tortoiseshell double-pointed needles with hallmarked silver protective guards; a Tyrolean two-colour carved wooden knitting-needle holder.

Equipment for crochet. (Top left-hand row, bottom to top) A U-shaped tool for hairpin crochet; a cardboard box of Penelope fine crochet hooks with bone handles; a large wooden hook; a small steel hook with a wooden handle; the sheath for the next object, a folding multi-hook, shown extended; a bone hook; a bone hook shaped like a rifle; two more bone hooks; and (above to the left) a packet of very fine steel hooks of the type used for the filet crochet in the square white mat. (Bottom right-hand row, bottom to top) Three patent metal hooks that slide back into handles for protection, one featuring a lighthouse; a metal hook in protective cover; another multi-hook in protective sheath; a hook with mother-of-pearl handle; a brass multi-hook,

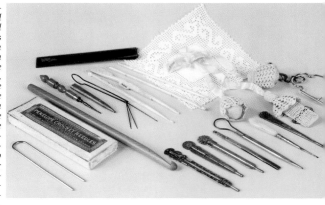

'The Shrimpton'; a crochet chatelaine with a needle-packet holder, pink silk pincushions and crochet-covered rings to hold safety pins; a metal spool-knave to hold a reel of thread.

Darning devices. (Back row, left to right) A wooden darner painted with a milkmaid; another with the words 'Darn those holes'; a stone darning egg; shaped wood with a handle; hand-carved with an owl handle; blue Bakelite, with two skeins of mending thread. (Front row, left to right) Two 'Marvel' darning devices, one upside down to show the label; a plain wooden glove darner and a polished wood example; another lying across a card of mending thread; a miniature stone egg glove darner; and a Cornish serpentine stone darner.

Crochet. There is also a variety of items connected with this craft. Crochet hooks were made in many sizes or materials according to the type of work for which they were used. They could be made in wood, bone, imitation tortoiseshell or plastic, while much smaller ones in

Right: *Perforated card for needlework items. (Clockwise from back centre) A green packet of 'Perforated Card Board' for needlework; a pink rectangular piece, and a two-coloured square, ready to be embroidered; a needlecase made from circular shapes, embroidered and with ribbon ties; a circular card and one with a flower design pricked out; an unworked rectangular card; a shape partly worked in red and green thread; a rectangular card, embroidered with a house, a tree and the message 'Home sweet home'. In the centre is a fragile needlecase made from punched card finished with blue ribbon and bearing the message 'Forget me not'.*

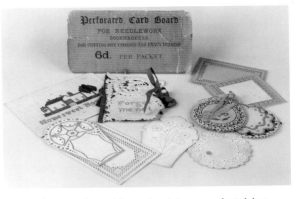

Left: *(Top to bottom) In a red container, a graduated dress bodice and leg-of-mutton sleeve pattern on fabric, made by Singer, 'price 2/6'; an oval wooden embroidery hoop fitted with a sample piece of broderie anglaise, with a label for genuine Madeira work; a round metal embroidery frame, photographed with a blue-edged handkerchief with typical Madeira embroidery of a girl in national costume, dating from the 1950s.*

Right: *A selection from many hundreds of packets of needles made by many different makers.*

Below: *Needlework books and ephemera. (Top row, left to right) An original bill for goods from Thérèse de Dillmont, the French needlework supplier; a page headed 'Needlecraft' with a list of the contents of different issues of this magazine, price 2d; a green paper book, 'The Exhibition Knitting, Netting and Crochet Book', price one penny, with a line illustration of the front of the Crystal Palace on the cover; a hardback 'Book of Stitches' by Ellen T. Masters; a small blue book with a gilt portrait of Queen Victoria on the cover, the 'Fancy Needlework and Embroidery Guide'. (Bottom row, left to right) 'The Encyclopedia of Needlework', by Thérèse de Dillmont; a small hardback book, 'Hart's Fancy-work Book'; a green paper booklet of patterns and another covered in dark leather; and a green paper booklet, a catalogue, 'Edgcomb's English, German and General Fancy Needlework No. 54'.*

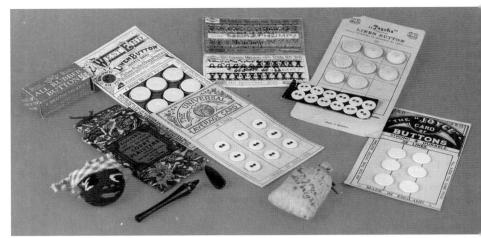

A collection of haberdashery and other sewing items. (Back, from far left) A red pack of all-rubber buttons; five cards of linen buttons and two cards of hooks and eyes, all featuring the makers' names. (Front from far left) A hand-made emery cushion in the form of a negro head with a check headscarf; a pack of court-plasters, for first aid for pricked fingers; a rosewood styptic pencil to stop bleeding from a prick; and a miniature sack filled with emery powder, with the message 'To keep your needles bright'.

A silver-plated spool-knave with a reel of cotton, and a pale blue glass silk winder.

steel, mostly with a protective device or cover, were used to make fine lace and other articles using fine crochet cotton. Some longer and larger hooks in the first mentioned materials were used for tricot work or Tunisian crochet. A crochet hook was used with a metal U-shaped tool to make an open type of crochet called hairpin crochet.

In addition to these specific collectors' items, much interest can be found in many of the haberdashery goods used in needlework, such as cards of decorative or linen or other useful buttons, usually with the maker's name, or cards of hooks and eyes or press studs. There is a huge variety of old cotton reels, made until the introduction of plastic reels in 1966. Needle packets are also a fascinating field, the extent of which will be revealed by a visit to the Forge Mill Needle Museum at Redditch, Worcestershire.

Lastly, old books on various aspects of needlework, including some delightful miniature ones, add interest to a collection. Many types of paper patterns for embroidery and other purposes were made, and even an occasional clothing pattern printed on fabric may be found.

FURTHER READING

ndere, Mary. *Old Needlework Boxes and Tools*. David & Charles, 1971.
aker, John. *Mauchline Ware*. Shire, 1985; reprinted 1998.
rears, Peter C. D. 'The Knitting Sheath', reprinted from *Folk Life*, in *A Journal of Ethnological Studies*, volume 20, 1981-2.
labburn, Pamela. *Beadwork*. Shire, 1980; reprinted 1994.
olby, Averil. *Pincushions*. Batsford, 1975.
roves, Sylvia. *The History of Needlework Tools and Accessories*. David & Charles, 1973.
artley, Marie, and Ingleby, Joan. *The Old Hand Knitters of the Dales*. Dalesman Books, 1978.
olmes, Edwin. *A History of Thimbles*. Cornwall Books, 1985.
olmes, Edwin. *Thimbles*. Gill & McMillan, Dublin, 1976.
orowitz, Estelle, and Mann, Ruth. *Victorian Brass Needlecases*. Needlework Treasures (Long Beach, California) and Thimble Collecting (Beverly, Maryland, USA), 1990.
ohnson, Eleanor. *Thimbles and Thimble Cases*. Shire, 1999.
1athis, Averil. *Antique and Collectible Thimbles and Accessories*. Collector Books (Kentucky, USA), 1986.
almer, Pam. *Tatting*. Shire, 1996.
into, F. and Eva. *Tunbridge and Scottish Souvenir Woodware*. Bell, 1969.
into, F. H. *Treen and Other Wooden Bygones*. Bell, 1969.
roctor, Molly. *Needlework Tools and Accessories: A Collector's Guide*. Batsford, 1990.
ogers, Gay Ann. *An Illustrated History of Needlework Tools*. John Murray, 1983.
aunton, Nerylla. *Antique Needlework Tools and Embroideries*. Antique Collectors Club, 1997.
hompson, Helen Lester. *Sewing Tools and Trinkets*. Collector Books (a division of Schroeder Publishing Co Inc). A book mainly of illustrations.
urner, Pauline. *Crochet*. Shire, second edition 1990.
Vhiting, Gertrude. *Old Time Tools and Toys of Needlework*. Dover Publications, 1971.

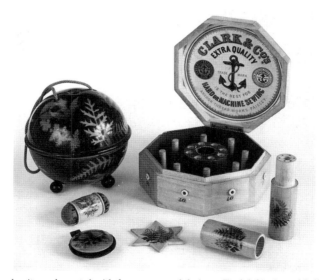

collection of wooden items decorated with fern or seaweed designs. (Back left) A wool-ball holder on ball feet, corated in dark brown with a lighter fern design; it has a hole in the top through which to pull the end of the ball om inside, and a cord carrying loop. (Back right) An octagonal cotton-reel box, the lid decorated with a fern design red and green; the inside has a label for Clark's Anchor thread; there are eight pegs to hold reels of different icknesses of thread, a central space for a thimble and holes for needles. (Bottom, left to right) A double-ended ncushion, with worn red velvet cushions, in a green and red fernware design; below, a small round pincushion corated with a seaweed pattern; a green and red fern-decorated star-shaped silk winder; and, shown open, a red id green fern-decorated container for tambour or fine crochet hooks (which are missing).

PLACES TO VISIT

Bethnal Green Museum of Childhood, Cambridge Heath Road, London E2 9PA. Telephone: 0181 983 5200 Fine collection of workboxes and caskets.

Birmingham Museum and Art Gallery, Chamberlain Square, Birmingham B3 3DH. Telephone: 0121 30. 2834. The Pinto Collection of wooden bygones. Website: www.brillsummer.org.uk

Cambridge and County Folk Museum, 2-3 Castle Street, Cambridge CB3 0AQ. Telephone: 01223 355159

Dales Countryside Museum, Station Yard, Hawes, Wensleydale, North Yorkshire DL8 3NT. Telephone 01969 667494. The Agar Collection of knitting sheaths.

Forge Mill Needle Museum and Bordesley Abbey Visitor Centre, Forge Mill, Needle Mill Lane, Riverside Redditch, Worcestershire B98 8HY. Telephone: 01527 62509.

Gawthorpe Hall (National Trust), Padiham, near Burnley, Lancashire BB12 8UA. Telephone: 0128. 771004. Good collection of needlework tools.

Gloucester Folk Museum, 99-103 Westgate Street, Gloucester GL1 2PG. Telephone: 01452 526467.

Guildford Museum, Castle Arch, Guildford, Surrey GU1 3SX. Telephone: 01483 444740. Website www.surreycc.gov.uk/guildford-museum

Museum of London, 150 London Wall, London EC2Y 5HN. Telephone: 0171 600 3699 extension 290.

Tudor House Museum, Bugle Street, Southampton, Hampshire SO14 2AD. Telephone: 01703 635904 Large collection of needlework tools.

York Castle Museum, Eye of York, York YO1 9RY. Telephone: 01904 613161. Website: www.york.gov.uk heritage/museums/castle

SOCIETIES

Dorset Thimble Society (for collectors of sewing tools everywhere). Membership secretaries. UNITED KINGDOM AND ELSEWHERE: Mrs Joan Mee, 8 St Michael's Road, Bournemouth, Dorset BH 5DX; telephone: 01202 555427. AUSTRALIA: Mr Jack Turner, 23 Harrow Road, Somerton Park South Australia 5044. UNITED STATES: Mrs Pat Rich, 4411 Walsh Street, Chevy Chase, Maryland MD 20815, USA.

Needlework Tool Collectors' Society of Australia, LPO Box 6025, Cromer, Victoria 3193, Australia.

Paper and card needlecases. (Top row, left to right). A brass-edged pink paper envelope with a colour print of shell containing a needle packet; a leather-covered snap-fastener case with various sizes of superior gold-eyed needle supplied by W. Woodfield & Sons and containing three original sheets of emery paper for removing rust fro. needles; a purse-shaped gold-decorated red leatherette case. (Bottom row, left to right) A small cardboard box fo packets of needles, inscribed 'Queen Victoria's Real Diamond Drilled Eyed Sharps, Richd Wyers Manufacture Redditch'; a paper needlebook with a painted wintry scene and the message 'A happy Christmas'; a book-shape cardboard box for packets of needles, the top decorated with the painted figure of a lady surrounded by gold pape lace.